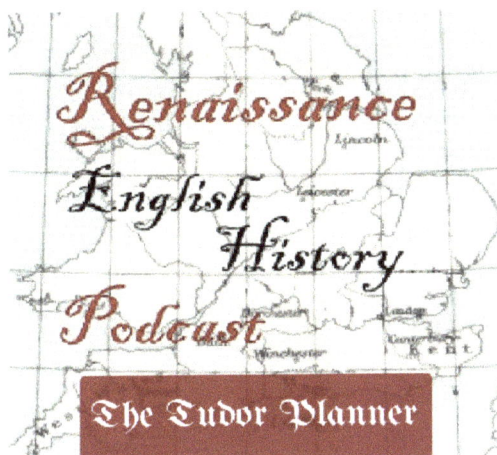

Renaissance English History Podcast

The Tudor Planner

2017

Monthly and Weekly Diary

If Found, please return to:

Name _____

Phone _____

Email _____

History Is More Than Dates!
Connect with the
Renaissance English History Podcast and
get the stories behind the people & events!

http://www.englandcast.com
facebook.com/englandcast
Heather Teysko - Podcaster and
Tudor Planner Creator

A note on music suggestions:
Each month has a musical CD listening suggestion.
You can find a Spotify playlist with each album at
http://spoti.fi/2eNYBYY

I hope you enjoy the soundtrack!

This is the first ever Tudor Planner! I can't wait to continue
improving it, and thank you for letting me be part of your life this
year! Please send your feedback to TudorPlanner@gmail.com

Goals for 2017

Health & Wellness

Creativity

Friends & Family

Spirit

Fun & Hobbies

January
2017

M	T	W	T	F	S	S
		December 2016	1	2	3	4
5	6	7	8	9	10	11
12	13	14	15	16	17	18
19	20	21	22	23	24	25
26	27	28	29	30	31	

January Goals

January 18, 1486 Henry VII weds Elizabeth of York, thus beginning the Tudor Dynasty

January Tasks

Monday	Tuesday	Wednesday
Listening Suggestion: Naked Byrd from the Armonico Consort		
2	3	4
9	10	11
16	17	18
23	24	25
30	31	1

Thoughts

M	T	W	T	F	S	S
February 2017		1	2	3	4	5
6	7	8	9	10	11	12
13	14	15	16	17	18	19
20	21	22	23	24	25	26
27	28					

Of all losses, time is the most irrecuperable for it can never be redeemed.

— Henry VIII

Thursday	Friday	Saturday	Sunday
			1
5	6	7	8
12	13	14	15
19	20	21	22
26	27	28	29
2	3	4	5

Doodles

February 2017

M	T	W	T	F	S	S
						1
2	3	4	5	6	7	8
9	10	11	12	13	14	15
16	17	18	19	20	21	22
23 / 30	24 / 31	25	26	27	28	29

January 2017

February Goals

February 11, 1531
Henry VIII granted the title of "Supreme Head of English church and clergy"

February Tasks

Monday	Tuesday	Wednesday
		1
6	7	8
13	14	15
20	21	22
27	28	1
6	7	8

Thoughts

M	T	W	T	F	S	S
March 2017		1	2	3	4	5
6	7	8	9	10	11	12
13	14	15	16	17	18	19
20	21	22	23	24	25	26
27	28	29	30	31		

It is not in the stars to hold our destiny but in ourselves.

– Shakespeare

Thursday	Friday	Saturday	Sunday
2	3	4	5
9	10	11	12
16	17	18	19
23	24	25	26
2	3	4	5
9	Listening Suggestion: Henry's Music: Motets from a Royal Choirbook from Alamire		

Doodles

March 2017

M	T	W	T	F	S	S
February 2017		1	2	3	4	5
6	7	8	9	10	11	12
13	14	15	16	17	18	19
20	21	22	23	24	25	26
27	28					

March Goals

March 24, 1603
Elizabeth I, the grand-
daughter of Henry VII,
dies

March Tasks

Monday	Tuesday	Wednesday
		1
6	7	8
13	14	15
20	21	22
27	28	29
3	4	5

Thoughts

M	T	W	T	F	S	S
		April 2017			1	2
3	4	5	6	7	8	9
10	11	12	13	14	15	16
17	18	19	20	21	22	23
24	25	26	27	28	29	30

An absolutely new idea is
one of the rarest things
known to man.
– Thomas More

Thursday	Friday	Saturday	Sunday
2	3	4	5
9	10	11	12
16	17	18	19
23	24	25	26
30	31	1	2
6	Listening Suggestion: Byrd: Lamentations, Four Part Mass/ Tallis: Lamentations I and II, etc. From the Choir of New College, Oxford		

Doodles

April 2017

M	T	W	T	F	S	S
March 2017		1	2	3	4	5
6	7	8	9	10	11	12
13	14	15	16	17	18	19
20	21	22	23	24	25	26
27	28	29	30	31		

April Goals

April 21, 1509
Henry, the second son of Henry VII and Elizabeth of York, becomes King of England

April Tasks

Monday	Tuesday	Wednesday
Listening Suggestion: Weelkes: Grant the King a Long Life from the Choir of Sidney Sussex College, Cambridge		
3	4	5
10	11	12
17	18	19
24	25	26
1	2	3

Thoughts

M	T	W	T	F	S	S
1	2	3	4	5	6	7
8	9	10	11	12	13	14
15	16	17	18	19	20	21
22	23	24	25	26	27	28
29	30	31		May 2017		

There is no greater
hell than to be a
prisoner of fear.
- Ben Johnson

Thursday	Friday	Saturday	Sunday
		1	2
6	7	8	9
13	14	15	16
20	21	22	23
27	28	29	30
4	5	6	7

Doodles

May
2017

M	T	W	T	F	S	S
		April 2017			1	2
3	4	5	6	7	8	9
10	11	12	13	14	15	16
17	18	19	20	21	22	23
24	25	26	27	28	29	30

May Goals

May 19, 1536
Anne Boleyn
executed at the
Tower of London

May Tasks

Monday	Tuesday	Wednesday
1	2	3
8	9	10
15	16	17
22	23	24
29	30	31
5	6	7

Thoughts

M	T	W	T	F	S	S
	June 2017		1	2	3	4
5	6	7	8	9	10	11
12	13	14	15	16	17	18
19	20	21	22	23	24	25
26	27	28	29	30		

Above our life we love a steadfast friend.
— Christopher Marlowe

Thursday	Friday	Saturday	Sunday
4	5	6	7
11	12	13	14
18	19	20	21
25	26	27	28
1	2	3	4
8	Listening Suggestion: Gibbons Church Music from the Choir of King's College, Cambridge		

Doodles

June
2017

M	T	W	T	F	S	S
1	2	3	4	5	6	7
8	9	10	11	12	13	14
15	16	17	18	19	20	21
22	23	24	25	26	27	28
29	30	31		May 2017		

June Goals

June 19, 1540
Thomas Cromwell
arrested and
imprisoned

June Tasks

Monday	Tuesday	Wednesday
Listening Suggestion: The Deer's Cry from The Sixteen		
5	6	7
12	13	14
19	20	21
26	27	28
3	4	5

Thoughts

M	T	W	T	F	S	S
		July 2017			1	2
3	4	5	6	7	8	9
10	11	12	13	14	15	16
17	18	19	20	21	22	23
24 / 31	25	26	27	28	29	30

I choose what I believe,
and say nothing.
For I am not as simple
as I may seem.
- Katherine of Aragon

Thursday	Friday	Saturday	Sunday
1	2	3	4
8	9	10	11
15	16	17	18
22	23	24	25
29	30	1	2
6	7	8	9

Doodles

July
2017

M	T	W	T	F	S	S
		June 2017	1	2	3	4
5	6	7	8	9	10	11
12	13	14	15	16	17	18
19	20	21	22	23	24	25
26	27	28	29	30		

July Goals

July 10, 1553
Lady Jane Grey pro-
claimed Queen
of England; she would
reign for nine days

July Tasks

Monday	Tuesday	Wednesday
Listening Suggestion: English Renaissnce from The King's Singers		
3	4	5
10	11	12
17	18	19
24	25	26
31	1	2

Thoughts

M	T	W	T	F	S	S
	1	2	3	4	5	6
7	8	9	10	11	12	13
14	15	16	17	18	19	20
21	22	23	24	25	26	27
28	29	30	31			August 2017

Though God hath raised me high, yet this I count the glory of my crown: That I have reigned with your loves.
- Elizabeth I

Thursday	Friday	Saturday	Sunday
		1	2
6	7	8	9
13	14	15	16
20	21	22	23
27	28	29	30
3	4	5	6

Doodles

August
2017

M	T	W	T	F	S	S
July 2017					1	2
3	4	5	6	7	8	9
10	11	12	13	14	15	16
17	18	19	20	21	22	23
24 / 31	25	26	27	28	29	30

August Goals

| |
| |
| |
| |
| |

August 8, 1588
England defeats the
Spanish Armada

August Tasks

| |
| |
| |
| |
| |

Monday	Tuesday	Wednesday
	1	2
7	8	9
14	15	16
21	22	23
28	29	30
4	5	6

Thoughts

M	T	W	T	F	S	S
		September 2017		1	2	3
4	5	6	7	8	9	10
11	12	13	14	15	16	17
18	19	20	21	22	23	24
25	26	27	28	29	30	

To be kind to all, to like many and love a few, to be needed and wanted by those we love, is certainly the nearest we can come to happiness.

– Mary Queen of Scots

Thursday	Friday	Saturday	Sunday
3	4	5	6
10	11	12	13
17	18	19	20
24	25	26	27
31	1	2	3
7	Listening Suggestion: John Taverner – Imperatrix Inferni – Votive Antophons from Alamire		

Doodles

September
2017

M	T	W	T	F	S	S
	1	2	3	4	5	6
7	8	9	10	11	12	13
14	15	16	17	18	19	20
21	22	23	24	25	26	27
28	29	30	31		August 2017	

September Goals

September 9, 1513 Battle of Flodden, killing most of Scotland's nobility, including King James IV

September Tasks

Monday	Tuesday	Wednesday
Listening Suggestion: From Tallis to Byrd from the Choir of Clare College, Cambridge		
4	5	6
11	12	13
18	19	20
25	26	27
2	3	4

Thoughts

M	T	W	T	F	S	S
		October 2017				1
2	3	4	5	6	7	8
9	10	11	12	13	14	15
16	17	18	19	20	21	22
23 / 30	24 / 31	25	26	27	28	29

Talking much is a sign of vanity, for the one who is lavish with words is cheap in deeds.
- Walter Raleigh

Thursday	Friday	Saturday	Sunday
	1	2	3
7	8	9	10
14	15	16	17
21	22	23	24
28	29	30	1
5	6	7	8

Doodles

October
2017

M	T	W	T	F	S	S
		September 2017		1	2	3
4	5	6	7	8	9	10
11	12	13	14	15	16	17
18	19	20	21	22	23	24
25	26	27	28	29	30	

October Goals

October 31, 1517
Martin Luther
nails the
95 Theses on the
Wittenberg church

October Tasks

Monday	Tuesday	Wednesday
Listening Suggestion: Thomas Tallis: Latin and English motets and anthems from the Rudolfus Choir		
2	3	4
9	10	11
16	17	18
23	24	25
30	31	1

Thoughts

M	T	W	T	T	S	S
November 2017		1	2	3	4	5
6	7	8	9	10	11	12
13	14	15	16	17	18	19
20	21	22	23	24	25	26
27	28	29	30			

It isn't that life ashore is distasteful to me. But life at sea is better.
— Francis Drake

Thursday	Friday	Saturday	Sunday
			1
5	6	7	8
12	13	14	15
19	20	21	22
26	27	28	29
2	3	4	5

Doodles

November
2017

M	T	W	T	F	S	S
						1
2	3	4	5	6	7	8
9	10	11	12	13	14	15
16	17	18	19	20	21	22
23 / 30	24 / 31	25	26	27	28	29

October 2017

November Goals

November Tasks

November 17, 1558
Mary I dies and
Elizabeth I ascends to the
throne: two formidable
female queens.

Monday	Tuesday	Wednesday
		1
6	7	8
13	14	15
20	21	22
27	28	29
4	5	6

Thoughts

M	T	W	T	F	S	S
		December 2017		1	2	3
4	5	6	7	8	9	10
11	12	13	14	15	16	17
18	19	20	21	22	23	24
25	26	27	28	29	30	31

Win hearts, and you have all
men's hands and purses.
— William Cecil

Thursday	Friday	Saturday	Sunday
2	3	4	5
9	10	11	12
16	17	18	19
23	24	25	26
30	1	2	3

Listening Suggestion: Joyne Hands: English Renaissance Music
from the Musicians of Swanne Alley

Doodles

December
2017

M	T	W	T	F	S	S
November 2017		1	2	3	4	5
6	7	8	9	10	11	12
13	14	15	16	17	18	19
20	21	22	23	24	25	26
27	28	29	30			

December Goals

December Tasks

December 31, 1558
Elizabeth I orders the
gospel, epistle, and litany
to be read in English

Monday	Tuesday	Wednesday
Listening Suggestion: As it fell on a Holie Eve from Parenthia		
4	5	6
11	12	13
18	19	20
25	26	27
1	2	3

Thoughts

M	T	W	T	F	S	S
1	2	3	4	5	6	7
8	9	10	11	12	13	14
15	16	17	18	19	20	21
22	23	24	25	26	27	28
29	30	31		January 2018		

Methinks love maketh men like angels.
- Catherine Parr

Thursday	Friday	Saturday	Sunday
	1	2	3
7	8	9	10
14	15	16	17
21	22	23	24
28	29	30	31
4	5	6	7

Doodles

December
26

Appointments

December
27

Appointments

December
28

Appointments

notes

December
29

Appointments

December
30

Appointments

December
31

Appointments

habit tracker	m	t	w	t	f	s	s

January
1

Appointments

January 1, 1515: King Henry XII of France dies and Charles Brandon escorts Mary Tudor home

January 2

Appointments

January 3

Appointments

January 4

Appointments

notes

January 5

Appointments

January 6

Appointments

January 7

Appointments

January 8

Appointments

habit tracker	m	t	w	t	f	s	s

January 2, 1492: The city of Granada in Spain falls to Ferdinand and Isabella, parents of Katherine of Aragon

January 9

Appointments

January 10

Appointments

January 11

Appointments

notes

January
12

January
13

January
14

habit tracker	m	t	w	t	f	s	s

January
15

Appointments

January 11, 1569: First lottery was drawn at St. Paul's Cathedral to raise money for Elizabeth I's government

January 16

Appointments

January 17

Appointments

January 18

Appointments

notes

January
19

Appointments

January
20

Appointments

January
21

Appointments

habit tracker	m	t	w	t	f	s	s

January 21, 1525: The Swiss Anabaptist movement is born, breaking a thousand years of church & state unity. Religious wars in Europe would impact each Tudor monarch in different ways

January
22

Appointments

January 23

Appointments

January 24

Appointments

January 25

Appointments

notes

January
26

January
27

January
28

habit tracker	m	t	w	t	f	s	s

January 25, 1533: King Henry VIII marries his second wife, Anne Boleyn, in secret

January
29

January 30

Appointments

January 31

Appointments

February 1

Appointments

notes

February 2

Appointments

February 3

Appointments

February 4

Appointments

habit tracker	m	t	w	t	f	s	s

January 31, 1547:
Henry VIII's death announced

February 5

Appointments

February 6

Appointments

February 7

Appointments

February 8

Appointments

notes

February 9

Appointments

February 10

Appointments

February 11

Appointments

habit tracker	m	t	w	t	f	s	s

February 7, 1478:
Sir Thomas More born

February 12

Appointments

February 13

Appointments

February 14

Appointments

February 15

Appointments

notes

February 16

Appointments

February 17

Appointments

February 18

Appointments

habit tracker	m	t	w	t	f	s	s

February 13, 1542:
Execution of Wife #5 Katherine Howard

February 19

Appointments

February 20

Appointments

February 21

Appointments

February 22

Appointments

notes

February 23

Appointments

February 24

Appointments

February 25

Appointments

habit tracker	m	t	w	t	f	s	s

February 25, 1570: Elizabeth I is
excommunicated by the Pope

February 26

Appointments

February
27

Appointments

February
28

Appointments

March
1

Appointments

notes

March 2

Appointments

March 3

Appointments

March 4

Appointments

habit tracker	m	t	w	t	f	s	s

March 5

Appointments

March 5, 1496: Henry VII enters the Exploration race commissioning the Cabots to explore the New World

March
6

Appointments

March
7

Appointments

March
8

Appointments

notes

March
9

March
10

March
11

habit tracker	m	t	w	t	f	s	s

March 9, 1566: David Rizzio, personal secretary to Mary Queen of Scots, is murdered in her presence

March
12

Appointments

March
13

Appointments

March
14

Appointments

March
15

Appointments

notes

March 16

Appointments

March 17

Appointments

March 18

Appointments

habit tracker	m	t	w	t	f	s	s

March 19

Appointments

March 16, 1534: The Church of England officially separates from the authority of the Pope

March
20

Appointments

March
21

Appointments

March
22

Appointments

notes

March 23

Appointments

March 24

Appointments

March 25

Appointments

habit tracker	m	t	w	t	f	s	s

March 24, 1603: Elizabeth I dies, possibly of lead poisoning from her makeup

March 26

Appointments

March
27

Appointments

March
28

Appointments

March
29

Appointments

notes

March 30

Appointments

March 31

Appointments

April 1

Appointments

habit tracker	m	t	w	t	f	s	s

March 30, 1533: Thomas Cranmer is appointed Archbishop of Canterbury

April 2

Appointments

April 3

Appointments

April 4

Appointments

April 5

Appointments

notes

April 6

Appointments

April 7

Appointments

April 8

Appointments

habit tracker	m	t	w	t	f	s	s

April 4, 1581: Francis Drake
knighted for sailing around the world

April 9

Appointments

April 10

Appointments

April 11

Appointments

April 12

Appointments

notes

April 13

Appointments

April 14

Appointments

April 15

Appointments

habit tracker	m	t	w	t	f	s	s

April 12, 1533: Thomas Cromwell becomes Chancellor of the Exchequer

April 16

Appointments

April 17

Appointments

April 18

Appointments

April 19

Appointments

notes

April 20

Appointments

April 21

Appointments

April 22

Appointments

habit tracker	m	t	w	t	f	s	s

April 23, 1564:
William Shakespeare is born (and died in 1616)

April 23

Appointments

April 24

Appointments

April 25

Appointments

April 26

Appointments

notes

April
27

Appointments

April
28

Appointments

April
29

Appointments

habit tracker	m	t	w	t	f	s	s

April
30

Appointments

April 24, 1546: Henry VIII charters the
English Navy; he loved building ships!

May
1

Appointments

May
2

Appointments

May
3

Appointments

notes

May 4

Appointments

May 5

Appointments

May 6

Appointments

habit tracker	m	t	w	t	f	s	s

May 2, 1536: Anne Boleyn and her brother
George Boleyn are both arrested

May 7

Appointments

May
8

Appointments

May
9

Appointments

May
10

Appointments

notes

May 11

Appointments

May 12

Appointments

May 13

Appointments

habit tracker	m	t	w	t	f	s	s

May 13, 1515: Princess Mary Tudor marries Charles Brandon

May 14

Appointments

May
15

Appointments

May
16

Appointments

May
17

Appointments

notes

May
18

May
19

Appointments

May
20

Appointments

habit tracker	m	t	w	t	f	s	s

May 19, 1536:
Anne Boleyn is executed

May
21

Appointments

May 22

Appointments

May 23

Appointments

May 24

Appointments

notes

May 25

Appointments

May 26

Appointments

May 27

Appointments

habit tracker	m	t	w	t	f	s	s

May 25, 1551: A huge earthquake hits London; events like this were often seen as omens

May 28

Appointments

May 29

Appointments

May 30

Appointments

May 31

Appointments

notes

June
1

Appointments

June
2

Appointments

June
3

Appointments

habit tracker	m	t	w	t	f	s	s

June 1, 1533:
Anne Boleyn is crowned Queen in London

June
4

Appointments

June 5

Appointments

June 6

Appointments

June 7

Appointments

notes

June 8

Appointments

June 9

Appointments

June 10

Appointments

habit tracker	m	t	w	t	f	s	s

June 7, 1520: Field of Cloth of Gold begins - Summit between Henry VIII and Francis I

June 11

Appointments

June
12

Appointments

June
13

Appointments

June
14

Appointments

notes

June
15

Appointments

June
16

Appointments

June
17

Appointments

habit tracker	m	t	w	t	f	s	s

June 12, 1553: Knowing he is dying, Edward VI names Lady Jane Grey his heir to prevent his Catholic sister Mary from inheriting

June
18

Appointments

June 19

Appointments

June 20

Appointments

June 21

Appointments

notes

June
22

Appointments

June
23

Appointments

June
24

Appointments

habit tracker	m	t	w	t	f	s	s

June 23, 1553: English ships set out in search of a Northeast Passage; instead they would find a sea route to Moscow

June
25

Appointments

June 26

Appointments

June 27

Appointments

June 28

Appointments

notes

June 29

Appointments

June 30

Appointments

July 1

Appointments

habit tracker	m	t	w	t	f	s	s

June 28, 1491:
Henry VIII is born

July 2

Appointments

July 3

Appointments

July 4

Appointments

July 5

Appointments

notes

July 6

Appointments

July 7

Appointments

July 8

Appointments

habit tracker	m	t	w	t	f	s	s

July 6, 1553:
Edward VI dies, age 15

July 9

Appointments

July
10

July
11

July
12

Appointments

Appointments

Appointments

notes

July 13

Appointments

July 14

Appointments

July 15

Appointments

habit tracker	m	t	w	t	f	s	s

July 16, 1546: Anne Askew is burned at the stake, one of the last religious martyrs of Henry VIII's reign

July 16

Appointments

July
17

July
18

July
19

Appointments

Appointments

Appointments

notes

July 20

Appointments

July 21

Appointments

July 22

Appointments

habit tracker	m	t	w	t	f	s	s

July 19, 1545: The English Navy fights the French Navy off the Isle of Wight: The Mary Rose sinks

July 23

Appointments

July 24

Appointments

July 25

Appointments

July 26

Appointments

notes

July 27

Appointments

July 28

Appointments

July 29

Appointments

habit tracker	m	t	w	t	f	s	s

July 30

Appointments

July 28 1540: Thomas Cromwell is executed while
Henry marries Katherine Howard

July
31

August
1

August
2

Appointments

Appointments

Appointments

notes

August 3

Appointments

August 4

Appointments

August 5

Appointments

habit tracker	m	t	w	t	f	s	s

August 3, 1553: Queen Mary triumphs over Lady Jane Grey's rebellion and enters London

August 6

Appointments

August 7

Appointments

August 8

Appointments

August 9

Appointments

notes

August 10

Appointments

August 11

Appointments

August 12

Appointments

habit tracker	m	t	w	t	f	s	s

August 13

Appointments

August 8, 1503: Princess Margaret Tudor marries the Scottish King James IV; the Stuart line descends from her

August 14

Appointments

August 15

Appointments

August 16

Appointments

notes

August 17

Appointments

August 18

Appointments

August 19

Appointments

habit tracker	m	t	w	t	f	s	s

August 16, 1531: Thomas Bilney was burned for distributing Tyndale's English Bible

August 20

Appointments

August 21

Appointments

August 22

Appointments

August 23

Appointments

notes

August 24

Appointments

August 25

Appointments

August 26

Appointments

habit tracker	m	t	w	t	f	s	s

August 24, 1572: St. Bartholemew's Day
Massacre killing Protestants in Paris

August 27

Appointments

August 28

Appointments

August 29

Appointments

August 30

Appointments

notes

August
31

Appointments

September
1

Appointments

September
2

Appointments

habit tracker	m	t	w	t	f	s	s

September 1, 1532: Anne Boleyn is made the Marquess of Pembroke

September
3

Appointments

September 4

September 5

September 6

notes

September
7

Appointments

September
8

Appointments

September
9

Appointments

habit tracker	m	t	w	t	f	s	s

September 7, 1533: Princess Elizabeth Tudor is born to Anne Boleyn

September
10

Appointments

September 11

Appointments

September 12

Appointments

September 13

Appointments

notes

September
14

September
15

September
16

habit tracker	m	t	w	t	f	s	s

September
17

September 16, 1541: Henry VIII arrives in York to meet with James V, but the meeting never happens

September 18

Appointments

September 19

Appointments

September 20

Appointments

notes

September
21

Appointments

September
22

Appointments

September
23

Appointments

habit tracker	m	t	w	t	f	s	s

September
24

Appointments

September 20, 1486: Arthur Tudor, the first son of Henry VII and Elizabeth of York, is born

September 25

Appointments

September 26

Appointments

September 27

Appointments

notes

September
28

Appointments

September
29

Appointments

September
30

Appointments

habit tracker	m	t	w	t	f	s	s

October 1, 1553: Queen Mary I, daughter of Henry VIII
and Katherine of Aragon, is crowned

October
1

Appointments

October
2

Appointments

October
3

Appointments

October
4

Appointments

notes

October 5

Appointments

October 6

Appointments

October 7

Appointments

habit tracker	m	t	w	t	f	s	s

October 5, 1553: Queen Mary I's first parliament declares her birth, and her parents' marriage, legitimate

October 8

Appointments

October
9

Appointments

October
10

Appointments

October
11

Appointments

notes

October
12

Appointments

October
13

Appointments

October
14

Appointments

habit tracker	m	t	w	t	f	s	s

October
15

Appointments

October 9, 1536: The Pilgrimage of Grace begins as a revolt against changes in the Church

October
16

October
17

October
18

Appointments

Appointments

Appointments

notes

October 19

Appointments

October 20

Appointments

October 21

Appointments

habit tracker	m	t	w	t	f	s	s

October 16, 1555: Hugh Latimer, a leading Protestant reformer, burned under Mary Tudor

October 22

Appointments

October 23

Appointments

October 24

Appointments

October 25

Appointments

notes

October 26

Appointments

October 27

Appointments

October 28

Appointments

habit tracker	m	t	w	t	f	s	s

October 24, 1537: Jane Seymore dies after complications from giving birth to Edward, Henry's longed-for son

October 29

Appointments

October
30

Appointments

October
31

Appointments

November
1

Appointments

notes

November
2

Appointments

November
3

Appointments

November
4

Appointments

habit tracker	m	t	w	t	f	s	s

November
5

Appointments

October 30, 1485: King Henry VII crowned King of England after defeating Richard III at Bosworth

November 6

Appointments

November 7

Appointments

November 8

Appointments

notes

November
9

November
10

Appointments

November
11

Appointments

habit tracker	m	t	w	t	f	s	s

November
12

Appointments

November 9, 1569: Revolt of the Northern Earls, an uprising of Catholics, begins to replace Elizabeth with Mary Queen of Scots

November
13

Appointments

November
14

Appointments

November
15

Appointments

notes

November
16

Appointments

November
17

Appointments

November
18

Appointments

habit tracker	m	t	w	t	f	s	s

November 14, 1501: Prince Arthur
Tudor marries Katherine of Aragon

November
19

Appointments

November 20

Appointments

November 21

Appointments

November 22

Appointments

notes

November
23

Appointments

November
24

Appointments

November
25

Appointments

habit tracker	m	t	w	t	f	s	s

November
26

Appointments

November 20, 1543: Famous Tudor portrait artist
Hans Holbein dies from plague

November 27

Appointments

November 28

Appointments

November 29

Appointments

notes

November
30

Appointments

December
1

Appointments

December
2

Appointments

habit tracker	m	t	w	t	f	s	s

November 30, 1554: St. Andrew's Day; England reconciled to the Catholic Church under Mary I

December
3

Appointments

December
4

Appointments

December
5

Appointments

December
6

Appointments

notes

December
7

December
8

December
9

habit tracker	m	t	w	t	f	s	s

December 8, 1542: Mary Queen of Scots, future rival to Elizabeth, is born; she was crowned Queen of Scotland at six days old when her father died

December
10

December
11

Appointments

December
12

Appointments

December
13

Appointments

notes

December 14

Appointments

December 15

Appointments

December 16

Appointments

habit tracker	m	t	w	t	f	s	s

December 16, 1485:
Katherine of Aragon is born to Ferdinand and Isabella

December 17

Appointments

December
18

Appointments

December
19

Appointments

December
20

Appointments

notes

December 21

Appointments

December 22

Appointments

December 23

Appointments

habit tracker	m	t	w	t	f	s	s

December 23, 1546: Henry VIII gives his last speech to Parliament

December 24

Appointments

December
25

Appointments

December
26

Appointments

December
27

Appointments

notes

December
28

December
29

Appointments

December
30

Appointments

habit tracker	m	t	w	t	f	s	s

December 27, 1539: Anne of Cleves
arrives at Deal to marry Henry VIII

December
31

Appointments

Notes

Notes

Notes

Notes

Notes

Notes

Notes

Notes

Notes

Notes

Notes

Notes

About

Heather created the Renaissance English History Podcast in 2009 to share and celebrate her love of 16th century England, making it one of the oldest continuously running indie history podcasts.. Episodes come out twice monthly, and you can subscribe on iTunes, any podcasting service, or listen online at http://www.englandcast.com

She is also the author of the novel *Sideways and Backwards, a Novel of Time Travel and Self Discovery*. Order on Amazon, iBooks, or find links at http://www.sidewaysandbackwardsbook.com

She leads several tours each year to England that focus on history and music. Learn more at http://www.englandcast.com/tours

Finally, she teaches others how to create and launch podcasts, and self publish books through online courses and coaching. You can find out more about her work at http://www.heatherteysko.com

Contact her via email: hello@heatherteysko.com twitter: @teysko Facebook.com/englandcast

www.ingramcontent.com/pod-product-compliance
Lightning Source LLC
Chambersburg PA
CBHW041934260326
41914CB00010B/1299